The Ultimate Guide to Exciting Low Carb Recipes

Exotic Flavours

MARIE SAMA LITUMBE AND LYDIA SAMA NSUTEBU

ISBN: Softcover   978-1-5434-9428-0
        Hardcover   978-1-5434-9429-7
        EBook   978-1-5434-9430-3

Print information available on the last page

Rev. date: 07/15/2019

To order additional copies of this book, contact:
Xlibris
0800-056-3182
www.xlibrispublishing.co.uk
Orders@ Xlibrispublishing.co.uk

This book is dedicated to our wonderful dad, Mr John Manga Sama of blessed memory, who instilled in us the value of family unity.

To our loving mom, Mrs Margaret Nkeng Sama, who from a very early age made us believe that cooking was fun and not a chore.

To our great brothers—Robby, Ernest, and Valentine—for all the quality time we spent together in our blessed home.

To our wonderful kids—Embelle, Mafany, Manga, Kelly, Emma, and Sidi—who make life a joy to live.

To our vast extended family and friends for being there.

To all the members of Exotic Flavours and Fitness, those we have inspired and those who have inspired us.

Finally, to the loves of our lives, Mafany Litumbe and Emmanuel Nsutebu, thank you for your endless love, encouragement, and support.

Contents

Lydia's Preface

It is a cold Wednesday morning, and my mum and I are sitting down in a doctor's room in the central hospital of Yaoundé, Cameroon. It is the early eighties, and this is the day I have been waiting for all my life—a day I thought would put an end to my predicament. But all my hopes are dashed, and my world crumbles at my feet when the doctor says what he has to say. 'Sorry, my dear, I will not grant you an exemption certificate from sports. You need to exercise. Exercise is good for you.' I am disillusioned, heartbroken, and I cry all the way back home. I am about twelve.

I grew up a very bubbly child, full of life and happiness, until I went to secondary school and became aware of my body image. If you were with me then, you would have seen a child who was over-weight. I struggled with exercise, and hated sports. I had an intense dislike for running. I was always out of breath and amongst the last in sports lessons. Life was hard, but I had hoped that a medical certificate would exempt me from doing sports at school. Unfortunately, this was not to be.

The years rolled by, and I continued to struggle with an image I didn't like. I didn't know how to help myself. I knew there was a problem, but I didn't have a solution. My sister Marie, who is co-author of this book, was also experiencing similar challenges with her own weight. It was consoling to have her share the same struggles. Sometimes we would laugh at people's nasty comments about us, even though they hurt deeply. To rub salt into the wound, some of the comments didn't come from afar; they came from close family members.

Then one Saturday afternoon, Marie, came home on holiday. (she was a university student at the time) That night, we talked non-stop and barely slept. We always had so much to talk about. It was during that night that she gave me some vital weight loss tips. You see, she had been chatting with a friend whose weight loss transformation had been rather dramatic. This friend emphasised the importance of healthy nutrition and exercise. I grabbed this PIECE of information from my sister and ran with it, and I am still 'running' until now.

My healthy lifestyle journey started with short walks, then gentle jogging, and finally running. I increased my distance progressively and I ate plenty of fruits and vegetables. It was exciting to see that one could lose weight as a result of the things one ate and by exercising. The amazing results I achieved was my driving force, and before long, friends started contacting me to find out what I had done to lose weight. This inspired me, and I wanted to help change others.

Nutrition is a very important element in a healthy lifestyle: you become what you eat. From a very young age, Marie and I had a passion for cooking, and this has helped to facilitate our healthy lifestyle journey. We are always working on and exchanging recipes. If we enjoy eating something, we do not rest until we can reproduce it. We are a work in progress when recipes are concerned.

I must give some credit to our mum for her upbringing techniques. When we were young, she would make us do chores and cook despite employing domestic help, it certainly paid off.

As years went by, I had a deep urge to help more people achieve their weight loss goals and live healthy lifestyles. My greatest desire was to share this message with as many friends and family members as possible. This is how the seed to write this book was planted. It is a dream I have nursed over the years. Last year my urge to share healthy lifestyle tips led me to create a group in Facebook called Exotic Flavours and Fitness. On this platform, like-minded people come together to share, support, and encourage one another to pursue healthy lifestyles. Many friends wanted to know what Marie and I did to lose weight and to maintain a healthy lifestyle. There was a constant demand for recipes as well as exercise tips. Creating Exotic Flavours and Fitness was a quick and easy way to reach out to many people. And following this up with a book is a dream come true.

I feel really happy and humbled when I get feedback from people who say that we have changed their lives and that we are an inspiration to many. My greatest joy, however, lies in the fact that people never believe me when I tell them my age. Oftentimes when I go to the gym with my eldest daughter, the person at the till would charge me a student rate because they think my daughter and I are school mates. Similarly, when I took her to her university interview, I was mistaken for an applicant and pointed in the wrong direction (this memory makes me smile).

The most exciting incident occurred a couple of months ago. I went into a shop to buy a cake tester. I was in a rush because my car park ticket was running out. I picked up the item and took it to the till; there was a long queue and no self-checkout facility. I started to panic at the thought of a parking fine. When it got to my turn, I handed over the money and cake tester to the lady with a sigh of relief. This lady however refused to sell it to me without proof of identity. She said she was not allowed to sell sharp items to people under the age of twenty-five. She added that she would need authorisation from the manager if I did not have proof of identity. At this point, I was having mixed emotions. Anxious at the thought of a parking fine, yet flattered by the fact that I seem to be ageing gracefully. This incident happened on the 1st September 2018, barely two days to my forty-ninth birthday. It is an incredible feeling.

I am grateful for the fact that today, I can walk, jog and run for ten miles and more at a stretch. I have done challenges where I did a minimum of ten miles every day for ten days, as well as over three hundred miles in one month. I am thrilled at the fact that I sometimes run to raise money for good causes. Looking back, I think I have come a very long way, and this could be you. I agree with Lao Tzu that 'the journey of a thousand miles begins with one step'.

Marie's Preface

Lydia and I have been cooking from a very early age. I have memories of us going to a little kiosk not too far from where we lived to buy two spoons of margarine at a time, since we couldn't afford a whole tub of 250 grams. We were both under the age of ten. We would get home and rub the fat into a tiny amount of flour in order to obtain our little dough. I even remember us baking our cakes in these huge metal pots with sand, but when the sand found its way into our cakes, we learnt that we could replace the sand with a saucer.

We got our recipes from anywhere and everywhere we possibly could. If we ever ate something nice whilst out, we would make an appointment with whoever prepared the meal so that we could be present when next they cooked that same meal. It didn't end there. Lydia and I wouldn't rest until we had put into practice what we had learnt, perfected the recipe and made it our own. Looking back now, I think that cooking is a gift that the good Lord blessed us with.

When I got to high school, I found myself suddenly getting out of shape. I really didn't understand what had gone wrong, and I had no one to help me deal with the problem at hand. Everybody simply greeted me with shock whenever they saw me. I remember when one of my older cousins was visiting home from America, and the first thing she said to Lydia and I when she saw us was 'Ah, you two are just turning into little guinea pigs'. My sister and I were very hurt, but we really had no idea as to how to help ourselves.

When I went to university in 1985, there was a close friend of mine who had been quietly working on her weight, and I was amazed when I saw her for the first time after three months. I immediately sought out her advice, and this was the first time that anyone had told me exactly what to do with regards to losing weight. Her diet consisted of plenty of fruits and vegetables, no sugar, and no oil; with plenty of exercise. This day marked the beginning of my weight loss journey.

My new-found passion for a healthy lifestyle is what led me to open my own gym in Douala in 1996 and Lydia and I ran it together until she left for the UK in 1999. The gym was operational for over sixteen years. What we understood over this period of time was that while exercising would keep you fit and healthy; your diet is what helped you lose weight. In other words, 'you get fit in the gym, and you lose weight in the kitchen'. Eighty percent of weight loss is completely dependent on your diet.

In October 2017, Lydia decided to create a group on Facebook called Exotic Flavours and Fitness. This group was simply a means of connecting with our friends all over the world who had an interest in living a healthy lifestyle. As the group's membership gradually increased, we found the need to educate people on cellular nutrition, especially since this was a topic that is very rarely covered in our local schools. We also had many friends who didn't know what to eat while living a low-carb lifestyle. This is what gave birth to the idea of a healthy cookbook. With this cookbook, we will finally be able to reach out to and educate people all over the world.

HOW A LOW-CARB LIFESTYLE HELPS IN WEIGHT LOSS

The human body is a carbohydrate-burning machine. In other words, our body gets its fuel from carbohydrates. Decreasing your carbs will cause your body to burn stored fat for energy. You are therefore transforming your body from a carbohydrate-burning machine into a fat-burning machine. This lifestyle ultimately leads to weight loss.

It is important to remember that this lifestyle does not focus on your daily calories. Decreasing your carbs lowers your insulin levels. According to Dr Atkins, one is only allowed twenty grams of carbohydrates during the first phase of one's high-protein diet. When your body hits ketosis (when the body starts metabolizing fat and converting it into ketones), you can then increase your carbs to thirty grams. It is very important to get your body to this stage because all the fat that has been stored over the years are being burned now; hence, you start losing weight immediately.

Cold Starters

HAM ROLLS

Ingredients

300 g thinly sliced ham
400 g peas
2 tbsp mayonnaise
1/4 tsp sugar
1 tsp vinegar
2 small tomatoes
Lettuce

Method

1. Mix mayonnaise, sugar and vinegar together in a bowl. Then add peas to the mixture.
2. Slice lettuce and lay on a tray.
3. Roll mixture in ham and lay on tray.
4. Place any leftover peas as demonstrated on the tray and garnish with tomatoes.

MIXED SALAD

Ingredients

1 cup grated carrots
1 cup sliced hard-boiled eggs
1 cup diced tomatoes
1 cucumber, sliced
1 cup sliced cabbage
50g of grated cheese for garnishing

Dressing

1/2 cup mayonnaise
1/2 cup plain yogurt
1 tsp sugar
1 tsp Dijon mustard
1/4 tsp salt
1/4 tsp white pepper
1/8 cup finely chopped onion

Method

1. Place all ingredients stylishly on a tray as seen in the picture.
2. Mix Salad dressing in a bowl.
3. Serve on a plate and add salad dressing if needed.

COLD-CUT SALAD

Ingredients

500 g beef, boiled
100 g salami
100 g ham
100 g smoked garlic sausage
100 g pork brawn
8 large pickles
1 large onion
1 cup sliced parsley
1/3 cup olive oil

Method

1. Slice all ingredients into thin strips.
2. Mix everything thoroughly in a bowl, add oil and mix again.

COLESLAW

Ingredients

1/2 cup mayonnaise
1/2 cup plain yogurt
1 tsp sugar
1/2 tsp dry mustard
A pinch of salt
A pinch of white pepper
4 cups finely shredded cabbage
1/2 cup shredded carrots
1/4 cup chopped onion

Method

1. Mix yogurt, mayonnaise, sugar, mustard, salt, and white pepper in a large bowl.
2. Add cabbage, carrot, and onion to the mixture and toss thoroughly.
3. Garnish with cucumber and carrots.

AVOCADO, SHRIMP, AND TOMATO SALAD

Ingredients

1 large avocado, diced
1 kg shrimps, peeled and deveined
2 tomatoes, diced
3 cloves of garlic, crushed

1 tbsp fish sauce
1/2 tsp white pepper
1 tbsp butter
Salt

Dressing

Thousand Island Dressing (about 6 tbsp)

Method

1. Season shrimps with white pepper, garlic, fish sauce, and salt. Allow to marinate for an hour in the refrigerator.
2. In a frying pan, melt butter and add shrimps. Cook shrimps for about 3 minutes on each side. Drain and allow to cool.
3. Add two tablespoons of Thousand Island Dressing on shrimps, avocado, and tomatoes in three separate bowls.
4. Arrange shrimps neatly in the centre of a tray, followed by the avocado and then the tomatoes.

QUINOA, PRAWN, AND AVOCADO SALAD

Ingredients

100g cooked prawns, chopped (leave a few whole)
1/2 cup cooked quinoa
1 red pepper, roasted, skinned, and sliced into strips
1 medium onion, finely chopped
1 tomato, chopped
2 tsp parsley, chopped

2 crushed garlic
1 spring onion, chopped
1 ripe avocado, chopped
2 tsp vinegar
Pinch of lemon rind (optional)
salt to taste
olive oil

Method

1. Put all ingredients in a large bowl except the quinoa, the red pepper, and a couple of whole prawns.
2. Mix them up well.
3. Place a food mould or pastry cutter on a plate.
4. Put the quinoa at the base, followed by the red pepper strips.
5. Next, put the avocado mixture and top with the whole prawns.
6. Carefully push it out of the mould.
7. Garnish with parsley and dust with paprika.

CABBAGE AND CARROT SALAD

Ingredients

2 cups of thinly sliced red cabbage
2 cups of thinly sliced white cabbage
2 cups of shredded carrots
Salt
Cucumber and tomatoes for garnishing

Dressing

4 tbsp olive oil
2 tbsp lemon juice
1/2 tsp salt
1 tbsp honey
1/2 tsp oregano

Method

1. Arrange carrot, white cabbage and red cabbage on a tray as seen in the picture above.
2. Mix together olive oil, lemon juice, salt, honey and oregano in a bowl.
3. Serve, add a drizzle of the dressing and enjoy.

AVOCADO, TOMATO, AND CUCUMBER SALAD

Ingredients

2 avocados, diced
4 medium tomatoes, chopped
1 cucumber, sliced
1 small onion, sliced
1 cup sliced lettuce

Dressing

2 tbsp olive oil
1 tbsp lemon juice
1/2 tsp salt
1/8 tsp black pepper
1/2 tsp oregano
1/8 tsp paprika

Method

1. Mix olive oil, lemon juice, salt, black pepper, oregano, and paprika in a bowl.
2. Pour the mixture over avocado, tomatoes, cucumber, onion, and lettuce and then toss everything to combine.

GIZZARD SALAD

Ingredients

1 kg gizzard
1 large onion
1 green pepper
3 cloves of garlic
1/3 cup chopped fresh basil
Salt
1/3 cup olive oil
1 yellow pepper
1 green pepper

Method

1. Slice gizzard lengthwise into three.
2. Blend onion, garlic, and basil.
3. Mix gizzard with blended ingredients and cook in a pot until tender. Allow juice to dry up, then add oil and allow to stir-fry for 5 minutes.
4. Serve on a tray and garnish with green and yellow peppers.

BELL PEPPER SALAD

Ingredients

4 assorted colours bell peppers
1 red onion
2 tbsp olive or sesame oil
2 tbsp lemon juice or vinegar
A pinch of salt

Method

1. Wash and dry the bell peppers.
2. Cut off their tops and remove the seeds.
3. Slice the peppers in strips and put in a large bowl.
4. Do the same for the onions.
5. Add the lemon juice or vinegar and salt, then mix well.
6. Drizzle the olive/sesame oil.
7. Serve with roasted fish/chicken or your preferred side.

AVOCADO TOPPED WITH SHRIMPS

Ingredients

2 large avocados
1 kg shrimps, peeled and deveined
2 tbsp fish sauce
2 cloves of garlic, crushed
1/2 tbsp black pepper
1 tsp salt
2 tbsp butter

Dressing

4 tbsp mayonnaise
1 tbsp tomato ketchup
1/4 tsp black pepper
1/8 tsp paprika

Method

1. Mix shrimps, fish sauce, garlic, black pepper, and salt in a bowl and allow to marinate for an hour.
2. Melt butter in a frying pan and cook shrimps for 3 minutes on each side.
3. Mix together the mayonnaise, paprika, tomato ketchup, and black pepper in a separate bowl. Add shrimps into the mixture.
4. Pile the shrimp mixture into the avocado halves.

SALSA SALAD

Ingredients

4 large tomatoes, diced
1/4 cup diced onion
1/2 cup chopped parsley
1 green pepper, diced
1 tbsp lemon juice
1/4 tsp black pepper
1 tbsp olive oil
1/2 tsp salt

Method

1. Mix tomatoes, onion, green pepper, and parsley in a bowl.
2. In a separate bowl, mix together olive oil, lemon juice, black pepper, and salt. Pour salad dressing over tomato mixture.

MACKEREL AND TOMATO SALAD

Ingredients

300 g mackerel
5 firm medium tomatoes, thinly sliced
1/4 cup chopped onion
1/4 cup chopped green pepper
1/4 cup chopped red bell pepper
Salt
White pepper
1 tbsp olive oil

Method

1. Season fish with salt and white pepper. Allow it to marinate for an hour in the refrigerator.
2. Fry fish and remove all the bones. Flake fish and add onion, green pepper, red bell pepper, and olive oil. Mix everything up and display as seen in the picture above.

BROCCOLI AND HAM ROLLS

Ingredients

Tender broccoli stems
Thinly sliced ham
Cream cheese

Method

1. Cook the broccoli stems until crisp and tender and pat dry with paper towels.
2. Mix the cream cheese in a small bowl.
3. Spread the cheese generously over the ham.
4. Place a couple of the broccoli stems on the ham, allowing the spears to protrude at one end. (You can trim down the stems.)
5. Roll up tightly. Repeat the process until you use up all the broccoli.
6. Serve immediately or keep in the fridge until ready to serve.

CUCUMBER AND CHEESE ROLL-UPS

Ingredients

Cucumber
Cream cheese
Plum or cherry tomatoes

Method

1. Mix the cream cheese to soften it.
2. Use a vegetable peeler to peel the cucumber into thin strips.
3. Spread the cheese on the cucumber strips and roll up tightly.
4. Seal with a tomato-garnished toothpick.
5. Serve immediately or refrigerate until ready to serve.

TUNA AND SWEET CORN CUCUMBER BOAT

Ingredients

1 or 2 large cucumber(s)
1/2 can of sweet corn (70g)
1 can of tuna (250g)
1 stalk of celery, thinly chopped
1 red pepper, thinly chopped
1/2 tsp white pepper

1 tbsp finely chopped onion
4 pieces of finely chopped sundried tomatoes
1 tbsp mayo (optional)
A pinch of salt
1 medium carrot for garnishing

Method

1. Slice the cucumber into two halves and then slice each half lengthwise.
2. Gently scrape out the inside with a spoon and discard the scooped seeds.
3. In a large bowl, mash up the tuna, then add the rest of the ingredients and mix well.
4. Scoop the tuna and sweet corn salad mixture into each cucumber half and *enjoy!*

Notes

Try to vary your salad mixture each time. You may also want to consider using chicken salad, Greek salad, or devilled egg mixture.

Hot Starters

If you must use sauces or seasoning cubes, ensure that they are low in sugar, low in salt and monosodium glutamate (MSG) free.

CHICKEN PEPPER SOUP

Ingredients

1 large chicken
1 large onion
1/4 cup chopped basil
1/4 cup chopped spring onions
1/2 tsp freshly ground ginger
Low sodium seasoning cube to taste

Salt to taste
30 g njansa (*Ricinodendron heudelotii*)
1 tsp bush pepper
Hot pepper sauce (optional)
1 medium tomato

Method

1. Chop the chicken into small pieces.
2. You can debone the chicken if you prefer to.
3. Season the chicken with onion, ginger, basil, spring onion, seasoning cube, and salt.
4. Cook until tender, then drain the stock and set aside to cool down.
5. When cold, transfer the stock to the fridge/freezer until the fat solidifies at the top. This can take a few hours.
6. In the meantime, dilute one seasoning cube in 750mlg of water.
7. Pour into a pot, then scrape off the solid fat from the chicken stock.
8. Discard the fat and add the neat chicken stock to the 750 ml water and allow to simmer.
9. Blend the njansa, tomato, and bush pepper, then sieve into the pot.
10. Add a pinch of water in the blender then repeat method 9.
11. Bring to a boil for about 5 minutes, then add the cooked chicken and allow to simmer for about 3 minutes.
12. Taste the soup and add salt to taste.
13. Serve hot and add some pepper sauce (optional).

SEAFOOD PEPPER SOUP

Ingredients

250 g prawns
250 g calamari
1tbsp sliced basil
1/4 cup sliced leeks
1/2 green pepper, crushed
2 crushed garlic cloves
1/2 onion sliced
Dry mushrooms, soaked in warm water
1/2 tsp white pepper
Salt

Method

1. Peel, devein, and slice prawns into little pieces.
2. Slice calamari into little pieces as well.
3. Mix them both in a bowl and season with garlic, white pepper, and salt. Allow to marinate for an hour in the refrigerator.
4. Pour two cups of water in a saucepan. Add the seafood mixture, leeks, basil, green pepper, garlic, onion, white pepper, mushrooms, and salt. Cook for 8–10 minutes max.

GOAT PEPPER SOUP

Ingredients

1 kg of meat, cut into small pieces
1 large onion, chopped
1 green pepper, crushed
1 tbsp sliced basil
3 cloves of garlic, crushed
1/4 tsp ground bush pepper
Salt
1 tbsp vegetable oil

Method

1. Season meat and boil until tender. Debone and return meat to the saucepan.
2. Add basil, onion, green pepper, bush pepper, garlic, salt, oil, and 1 1/2 cup of water. Cook for a further 10 minutes.

MIXED VEGETABLE SOUP

Ingredients

1 tbsp butter
1 cup diced carrots
1 cup cauliflower, cut into small pieces
1/2 onion, chopped
1/4 cup sliced celery
1/3 cup sliced leeks
1 cup chicken or beef broth
1/4 tsp white pepper
Salt to taste

Method

1. Melt butter in a pot and add onion. Fry for a minute and add leeks, celery, carrots, cauliflower, white pepper, and salt. Sauté for another minute and add beef/chicken broth, plus a cup of water. Boil for about 10 minutes and blend into a smooth soup. If you find the soup too thick, add some water.
2. Serve the soup hot.

BROCCOLI SOUP

Ingredients

1 tbsp olive oil
2 cloves garlic, chopped
1/2 onion, chopped
1 small green pepper, sliced
2 cups broccoli, cut into small pieces
1/3 cup sliced leeks
1/4 cup sliced celery
1 cup chicken or beef broth
Salt to taste
1/4 tsp white pepper

Method

1. Heat oil in a pot and add onion and garlic. Sauté for a minute and add green pepper, broccoli, leeks, celery, white pepper, broth, salt, and a cup of water.
2. Boil for about 10 minutes and blend into a smooth paste. Add more water if you find the soup too thick.

CREAMY CAULIFLOWER SOUP

Ingredients

1 tbsp butter
2 cloves of garlic, chopped
1/2 onion, chopped
2 cups cauliflower, cut into little pieces
1/2 tsp white pepper
Salt to taste
1 cup chicken stock
1/2 cup whipping cream (optional)
1/4 cup sliced leeks
1/4 cup sliced celery
1/4 cup sliced green pepper

Method

1. Melt butter in a pot and add onion and garlic. Sauté them for about a minute. Add cauliflower pieces, celery, leeks, green pepper, white pepper, salt, chicken stock, and a cup of water. Cook for over 8 minutes.
2. Blend everything to obtain a smooth paste. Return soup to the pot and add whipping cream. Stir over low heat for a further 5 minutes. If you find the soup too thick, you can add some water. Serve hot.

PUMPKIN SOUP

Ingredients

1 tbsp butter
1 cup chicken or beef stock
250 g boiled pumpkin
1/2 cup diced onion
2 garlic cloves, chopped
1/4 tsp white pepper
Salt to taste
1 tbsp grated cheese

Method

1. Melt butter in a saucepan and sauté onion and garlic for about a minute. Cut boiled pumpkin into cubes and add to the saucepan. Toss for a minute and add white pepper, salt, stock, and a cup of water.
2. Bring to boil for approximately 4 minutes and blend into a soup. Garnish with grated cheese and serve hot.

LIGHT MEAT SOUP

Ingredients

250 g meat
400 ml meat stock (you can add some water)
1 medium carrot, thinly diced
1 stalk of spring onion, chopped
1/2 tsp white pepper
Seasoning cube to taste
1 small onion, chopped
1 tsp freshly ground mixed herbs and spices (ginger, garlic, basil, parsley, and celery)
1 small tomato, grated
A pinch of salt
Hot pepper sauce (optional)

Method

1. Season and cook your meat until tender.
2. Chop the cooked meat into tiny pieces and set aside.
3. Bring the meat stock to a boil, then add the tomato, seasoning cube, white pepper, mixed spices and herbs.
4. Cover the pot and allow to boil on low to medium heat for about 3 minutes.
5. Taste and add a pinch of salt if required.
6. Add the meat, followed by the carrot and spring onion, and let it simmer for a minute or two.
7. Serve hot and enjoy!

Main Course

CHICKEN STIR FRY

Ingredients

600g skinless, boneless, chicken thigh
150g bean sprouts
200g sugar snaps or par boiled green beans
3 bell peppers thinly sliced (assorted colours)
1 large onion chopped
2-3 carrots diced
¼ cup fresh basil, sliced

½ teaspoon ground/grated ginger
1 tsp white pepper
3 cloves of garlic, ground
1 leek stalk chopped
1 tsp corn starch diluted in 3 tbsp of water (this will add some juice)
1 tbsp low sodium oyster sauce
Pinch of salt to taste
2 tbsp vegetable/olive oil

Method

1. Chop up the chicken and marinate in ginger, garlic, salt, white pepper for a couple of hours.
2. Heat the oil in a large wok/pan and cook the onion for about 2 minutes.
3. Add the chicken and cook on medium heat for about 6 minutes or until both sides are fully cooked.
4. Add the vegetables, the diluted corn starch and the oyster sauce, then cook until vegetables are crips and tender.

Serve hot and enjoy.

CAULIFLOWER PIZZA

Ingredients

For the Crust

2 cups grated cauliflower
1 cup grated mozzarella cheese (or cheese of your choice)
A pinch of salt
1 tsp mixed herbs
1/2 tsp garlic powder or 2 cloves crushed garlic
1/4 tsp white pepper
1 beaten egg

For the Filling

Tomato
Mushroom
Cooked prawns
Mixed bell peppers
Olives
Oregano
Grated mozzarella (enough to go around the crust)

Method
1. Preheat your oven to 190°C.
2. Line a baking tray with parchment paper.
3. Put your cauliflower in a bowl and microwave for 5 minutes, stirring halfway through.
4. When it cools down, transfer it on to a clean tea towel and wring out as much water as possible.
5. Put it back in a bowl and add the rest of the ingredients for the crust and mix well.
6. Put the mixture on the lined baking tray and shape into a pizza dough. Let the dough be 1/4-1/2 inch thick, and the edges a little higher. You can use your hands or a spoon.

7. Bake the crust until golden brown. This usually takes about 10 -15 minutes depending on your oven
8. Put the tomato sauce on the base, add the rest of the fillings, and top with cheese. Sprinkle some oregano or mixed herbs and return to a preheated oven until the cheese melts (approximately 5 minutes).

Tips

You can use any cheese of your choice, as well as change the toppings to suit you.
Ensure that the crust does not stick on the parchment paper before adding the toppings.
I sautéed my veggies before adding them to the crust. That way, they stayed moist and saved me time. My pizza was ready as soon as the cheese melted.

ASSORTED MEAT STIR-FRY

Ingredients

1/2 kg goat meat
1/2 kg beef
1/2 kg pork
1/2 kg tripe
1/2 kg cow intestine
1/2 cup vegetable oil
2 large onions, sliced
5 cloves of garlic, crushed
1/2 cup sliced basil
1/2 cup sliced leeks
1/2 cup sliced celery leaves
1 tsp freshly ground ginger
Salt to taste

Method

1. Season your meat and boil each type separately until tender.
2. Cut up the meat into little strips.
3. Heat oil in a wok and fry onion, tomatoes, and garlic for about 5–6 minutes or until the tomatoes are cooked.
4. Add the assorted meat, ginger, basil, leeks, celery, and salt. Stir-fry for another 5 minutes.

CHICKEN WITH BLACK MUSHROOMS

Ingredients

1 kg chicken fillets, cut into small pieces
1 onion, sliced
4 garlic cloves, crushed
1 tsp black pepper
3 tbsp soy sauce
2 tbsp sesame oil
1 tsp of freshly ground ginger
A handful of dried black mushrooms

Method

1. Season chicken with garlic, black pepper, soy sauce, ginger, and salt. Allow to marinate for an hour.
2. Heat oil in a heavy saucepan and fry onion for about a minute. Do not allow to get brown. Add the marinated chicken and stir from time to time until the chicken is cooked.
3. Soak the black mushrooms in warm water for 30 minutes. Drain and cut them into small pieces.
4. Add the black mushrooms to the already cooked chicken and stir.

FISH PARCEL

Ingredients

500 g boneless fish
1/2 tsp white pepper
3 spring onions, chopped
Salt to taste
1 tsp freshly squeezed lemon juice
(optional)
1/2 tsp paprika
1 tsp olive oil or sesame oil

Mixed bell peppers, cut into long strips
(julienne shapes)
Courgette/zucchini, thinly sliced
(approximately 8 slices)
1 onion, diced in chunks
Chili peppers (optional)
Parchment paper/baking paper/
Greaseproof paper large enough to
wrap up the fish and ingredients

Method

1. Preheat oven to 200°C.
2. Clean the fish and put in a bowl
3. Add the rest of the ingredients, except the veggies.
4. Place the parchment paper on a flat surface. Ensure that it is large enough for your parcel.
5. Line up the vegetables on the parchment paper, then put the fish on top of the vegetables.
6. Wrap up the fish into a parcel and place on a baking tray.
7. Put in the preheated oven, for about 10–15 minutes. Cooking time may vary depending on your oven or fish size.
8. Unwrap parcel and drizzle with sesame or olive oil. Enjoy!

CAULIFLOWER JELLOF

Ingredients

4 cups grated cauliflower
1 can mushrooms (400 g)
200 g bacon, sliced and fried until crispy
2 eggs, fried and cut into small pieces
1 cup diced carrots
200 g beef, boiled and cut into small pieces
1/2 cup sliced leeks
1/3 cup chopped onion
3 cloves of garlic, crushed
1/2 cup celery leaves
1/2 tsp white pepper
Salt
1/3 cup vegetable oil

Method

1. Cook cauliflower and carrots in beef stock for 5 minutes and then drain.
2. Pour oil in a wok and add onion, garlic, leeks, and celery. Allow to cook for 2 minutes.
3. Add cauliflower, mushrooms, bacon, eggs, white pepper, and salt. Toss thoroughly and serve.

GREENS (AMARANTHUS) WITH DRIED FISH

Ingredients

8 cups sliced greens
1 large onion, thinly sliced
3 medium tomatoes, chopped
1/2 cup lightly crushed crayfish
2 pieces dried fish
1/2 cup vegetable oil
Salt to taste

Method

1. Cook the vegetable in a pot of boiling water for a few minutes or until they're tender.
2. Drain all the water and set aside.
3. Heat oil in a heavy saucepan and add onion and tomatoes.
4. After about 5 minutes, add the dried fish and cook for another 5 minutes.
5. Add greens, crayfish, and salt and toss thoroughly. Allow to cook for further 5 minutes on low heat.

SAUTÉED PORK

Ingredients

1 kg pork, cut into small pieces
1 tsp freshly ground ginger
3 cloves of garlic, crushed
1 large onion, thinly sliced
1 celery stem plus leaves, sliced
1 large leek stem, sliced
Salt to taste
1/3 cup vegetable oil
Kankan (optional)

Method

1. Season pork with ginger, garlic, Kankan, salt, onion, celery, and leeks. Allow to marinate in the refrigerator for at least 2 hours.
2. Put the meat in a heavy saucepan and cook over low heat for a start. You can increase the heat after enough juice has been secreted.
3. When the pork is cooked, add oil and a tablespoon of Kankan for an extra twist. Allow pork to fry for 5 minutes.

OVEN-GRILLED BUTTERFLY CHICKEN

Ingredients

1 large chicken (2.5 kg)
1 tsp freshly ground ginger
1 tsp crushed garlic
2 tbsp freshly ground herbs (basil, parsley, and celery)
2 tbsp mustard (mild)
1 tsp crushed white pepper
1 tsp paprika
Seasoning cubes to taste. (we recommend low sodium and MSG free)
Salt to taste (for a large chicken, you might need 1/4 tsp)
Olive oil for brushing

Method

1. Spatchcock or butterfly your chicken (see tips below).
2. Score the chicken (use a sharp knife to make parallel shallow cuts through the skin).
3. Rub the salt and crushed seasoning cubes all over the chicken and set aside.
4. Put the rest of the ingredients in a bowl and mix well, forming a paste.
5. Generously rub the paste all over the entire chicken.
6. Cover and leave to marinate for a couple of hours or overnight.
7. Place on a grill rack, brush with oil, and put in the oven grill.
8. Let it cook for about 30 minutes or until golden brown at 180°C.
9. Turn over the chicken and let it cook for a further 20 minutes.

10. Adjust the heat accordingly so that it cooks thoroughly.
11. Remove from the oven when both sides are golden brown and the juice from the chicken is clear and not pink.

Tips

To spatchcock or butterfly a chicken means to take the backbone out of a whole chicken so that it opens flat. I prefer to butterfly my chicken from the front because I find it easier and do not have to struggle with taking the spine out. That way, the chicken remains whole.

Now place the chicken on its back, stomach side up, and cut through completely with a sharp knife. Next, flip the chicken over and press flat to butterfly it.

Score especially around the thick areas, like the breast and the thighs.

This chicken can be done on a charcoal BBQ, oven, or grill; and it can even be pot/pan-roasted. Cook on medium to low heat so that it cooks thoroughly.

OKRA SOUP (LADIES' FINGERS)

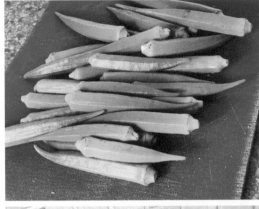

Ingredients

400 g chopped okra
300 g cooked meat
500 ml meat stock
1 bundle of sliced spinach
2 tbsp crayfish
1 seasoning cube
1 small onion, chopped
2 sticks of spring onions, chopped
A pinch of salt to taste

Method

1. Put the cooked meat in a pot and add the stock from the meat. You can top up the stock by adding water
2. Bring to a boil, then add the onion, crayfish, and spinach.
3. Let it boil for about 2 minutes then taste.
4. Add the seasoning cube and/or salt accordingly.
5. Finally, add the okra and cook till tender yet crunchy.
6. Taste again and make the necessary adjustments.
7. Serve with your favourite vegetable fufu. (Recipe in the book)

TIGER PRAWNS WITH GARLIC AND PARSLEY

Ingredients

1 kg prawns
3 cloves of crushed garlic
1 tsp white pepper
1/2 tsp salt
1 large onion, chopped
2 medium tomatoes, chopped
4 tbsp vegetable oil
1/4 cup chopped parsley
1 tbsp fish sauce

Method

1. Peel tiger prawns and devein.
2. Season with garlic, fish sauce, white pepper, and salt. Allow to marinate for an hour.
3. Pour the vegetable oil into a heavy saucepan and add the onion and tomatoes.
4. Cook for 10–15 minutes and then add the tiger prawns. Cook for 8–10 minutes. Put in the parsley a minute before you remove pot from the heat.

BROCCOLI JELLOF

Ingredients

4 cups sliced broccoli
1 can mushrooms (400 g)
1 cup diced carrots
200 g beef, sliced into small pieces after boiling
1 cup beef stock (250 ml)
1/2 cup sliced leeks
1/3 cup chopped onion
1/2 cup sliced celery leaves
1/2 tsp white pepper
1/4 cup oil

Method

1. Boil sliced broccoli and carrot in beef stock for about 5 minutes and then drain.
2. Pour oil into a wok and then add onion, leeks, and celery leaves. Toss them all together for 2 minutes.
3. Add broccoli, carrot, beef, mushrooms, white pepper, and salt to taste. Toss thoroughly for another 5 minutes and then remove from heat.

SOLE FILLET ROLLS

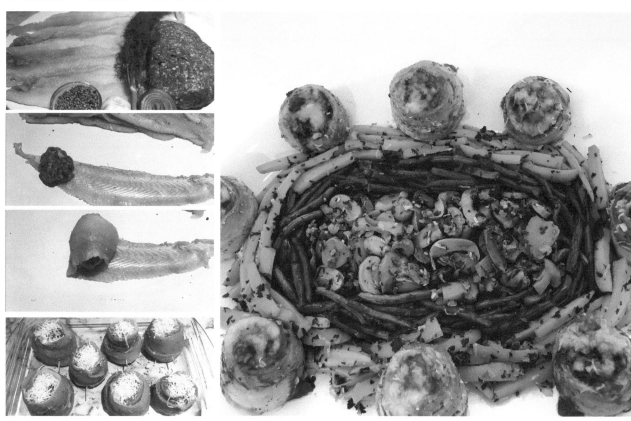

Ingredients

1 kg sole fillet
750 g minced beef
1 large onion
white pepper/black pepper
4 cloves of garlic, crushed
Salt
150 g grated mozzarella
Oregano
Fennel for garnishing (optional)

Method

1. Season the mincemeat with onion, oregano, salt, and black pepper.
2. Season the fish fillet with salt, white pepper, and garlic.
3. Shape the mincemeat into balls and roll the sole fillet around each ball. Use a toothpick to hold the end of the fish and top with grated cheese.
4. Grease your casserole and put the sole fillet rolls in it.
5. Cook in a preheated oven (180°C) for about 30 minutes or until the juice from the meat is clear.

CABBAGE ROLLS

Ingredients

1 large head of cabbage
1/2 kg mincemeat
1 large onion, thinly chopped (save 1/4 for tomato sauce)
4 cloves of crushed garlic (save 2 cloves for tomato sauce)

5 large basil leaves, sliced
1 tsp ground white pepper
3 tomatoes, chopped
1 cup mixed vegetable
Seasoning cube
Salt to taste

Method

1. Cut the centre core out of the cabbage and carefully place the cabbage in a large pot of boiling water (core facing downwards)
2. Allow to boil for about 15 minutes.
3. In a separate pot, make some tomato sauce by heating the oil and then adding in the onion, garlic, and tomatoes, respectively.
4. Cook for about 10 minutes, stirring from time to time.
5. Season the mincemeat with onion, garlic, white pepper, seasoning cube, and salt.
6. Add carrot and sweet corn and mix thoroughly.(optional)
7. Carefully remove whole leaves from cabbage, then place one heaped tablespoon of the meat mixture on each leaf and roll.
8. Place the rolled cabbage in a casserole dish. Pour the cooked tomato sauce on the rolls, then cover with foil.
9. Place in a preheated oven and cook for an hour.
10. Taste and adjust as required.

Note

If initially you do not get enough cabbage leaves, continue to put the cabbage in boiling water until you get the number required.

SPINACH IN TOMATO SAUCE

Ingredients

1 bag frozen Spinach (allow to thaw)
250g cooked meat + stock
1 seasoning cube
1 medium onion, chopped
2 tbsp crayfish
3 medium tomatoes
Salt to taste
Vegetable oil

Method

1. Squeeze out the water from the spinach.
2. Add the crushed seasoning cube and crayfish to the spinach and mix well.
3. Pour some oil in a pot and fry the onions for 2 minutes, while stirring.
4. Then add the tomatoes and continue to cook.
5. When the water starts to dry out, add some of the freshly cooked meat stock (approximately 50 ml). Do this in two batches.
6. Stir in the spinach and cook till the water dries out, but not until it is burnt.
7. Add salt to taste and serve.

Tips

You can use the same method to cook fresh spinach.

STUFFED MARROW/COURGETTE/ZUCCHINI

Ingredients

2 medium marrows
250 g cooked mincemeat (recipe in the book)
1 large chopped tomato or half a can

Grated mozzarella or preferred cheese
Mixed herbs
Salt to taste

Method

1. Preheat your oven to 180°C.
2. Add the tomato into the cooked mincemeat and cook until the water dries out.
3. Ensure that the mincemeat does not burn.
4. Wash and dry the marrows.
5. Cut it into two halves lengthwise.
6. Use a spoon and gently scoop the seeds out.
7. Spoon in the mincemeat mixture. Cover with foil and place in the oven.
8. Bake for 20 minutes or until marrow is tender.
9. Remove foil, top the marrow with cheese, and sprinkle with mixed herbs.
10. Bake uncovered until cheese melts and begins to turn brown.

Notes

A marrow is a courgette/zucchini that has been left on the plant to grow a little longer. A baby marrow is actually a courgette/zucchini.

The above recipe can therefore be used on courgettes as well as other vegetables.

PAN-GRILLED FISH (FILLET SALMON AND TUNA STEAK)

Ingredients

500g fish (cut into pieces)
1/2 tsp paprika
1/2 tsp white pepper
1 tbsp fish sauce (optional)
2 crushed garlic cloves
A pinch of salt to taste

Method
1. Put the pieces of fish in a bowl and add the other ingredients.
2. Leave to marinate for a couple of hours or overnight.
3. Preheat your griddle pan or skillet.
4. Wet the pan with a drizzle of olive oil.
5. Place the pieces of fish in the pan without overcrowding.
6. Cook on medium/high heat for about 2 minutes, then turn the fish over and cook for another 2 minutes or until the fish is cooked through.

Tip

This is a very quick, tasty, and easy way to cook fish. Try using any fish of your choice.

NO PASTA LASAGNE

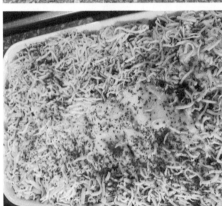

Ingredients

500 g cooked mincemeat as demonstrated in the book
250 g tomato sauce
250 g creamy sauce
1 medium onion, chopped
200 g mushrooms, sliced

300 g mozzarella cheese
Oregano or dried mixed herbs
1 medium courgette/zucchini, thinly sliced
1 aubergine, thinly sliced

Method

1. Preheat oven to 250°C.
2. Put the cooked mincemeat in a pot and add the tomato sauce.
3. Once it starts to simmer, add the mushrooms and cook for 2 minutes.
4. When it cools down, put a layer of the mincemeat in tomato sauce at the bottom of your dish, followed by the creamy sauce, mozzarella cheese, and herbs.
5. Cover the creamy sauce with the sliced courgette. Let them overlap one another so the creamy sauce is completely covered.
6. Repeat the process of the first layer: tomato sauce, creamy sauce, and then aubergine.
7. Now top up the last layer with tomato sauce, creamy sauce, cheese, and mixed herbs.
8. Cover with foil, then put in the oven for 1 hour or until vegetables are cooked.

Tips

Be flexible and try using other vegetables.
This lasagne can be cooked using tomatoes and creamy sauce from a jar, although we recommend that you make yours.
For a creamy sauce, follow instructions for béchamel sauce and simply add some cheese.

MINCEMEAT

Ingredients

500 g minced meat
1 onion, finely chopped
2 cloves of garlic, finely chopped
2 spring onions, chopped
1/2 tsp white pepper
1/4 tsp ground ginger

1/2 tsp ground basil
1/2 tsp ground celery
1 tsp mixed herbs
1 seasoning cube
Salt to taste

Method

1. Combine all the ingredients in a large pot.
2. Cook on low heat, stirring continuously, until the meat is brown.
3. Put in a colander to drain off any excess water/fat or continue stirring until water from the mincemeat dries off.

Tip

You do not need to add any water when cooking mincemeat. Allow it to cook in its own juice.

This can be used as a base for a variety of dishes, like lasagne, spaghetti bolognese, mince pasta bake, and many more.

MUSHROOM BÉCHAMEL SAUCE (CREAM SAUCE)

Ingredients

250 g sliced mushrooms
150 ml chicken stock
1 medium onion, chopped
300 ml double cream
2 tsp cornstarch or plain flour

2 cloves of crushed garlic
1/2 tsp crushed white pepper
2 tbsp butter
Salt to taste
1/4 tsp browning colour (optional)

Method

1. Melt the butter in a saucepan.
2. Add the garlic and onions and stir over low heat for a minute.
3. Blend in the cornstarch or flour and continue to stir. It will start to form a paste.
4. Pour in the chicken stock in bits and continue to stir.
5. Once it starts to boil, add the mushrooms and cook till tender.
6. Pour in the double cream, then add the white pepper and salt to taste.
7. Allow to simmer on low heat for about 2 minutes.

Notes

If you do not like the whitish/creamy colour, you can use browning colour to enhance the colour of the sauce.

OVEN-GRILLED TILAPIA AND MILK FISH

Ingredients

3 medium sized fish, cleaned and incised
1 tomato, grated
1 medium onion, grated
4 cloves of crushed garlic
2 tbsp ground ginger
10 medium basil leaves, ground

1 tsp paprika
2 seasoning cubes
Salt to taste
1/2 tsp white pepper
20 ml vegetable oil

Method

1. Mix together all the ingredients into a paste in a medium-sized bowl.
2. Season fish with the above mixture and allow to marinate for a couple of hours or overnight.
3. Place fish on a grill, brush with oil and wrap with foil.
4. Put in a preheated oven, and cook for approximately 30 minutes or until cooked.
5. For a crisp fish skin, remove foil after 30 minutes. Carefully drain any water, and return to the oven until golden brown.

Notes

This can also be done on a charcoal BBQ or pan griddle. Cooking times may vary.

STUFFED PORTOBELLO MUSHROOMS

Ingredients

4 large Portobello mushrooms
4 baby tomatoes, sliced in half
3 cloves of garlic, crushed
Mozzarella pearls/balls or grated
Mozzarella

Dried mixed herbs (optional)
A few fresh basil leaves, sliced
A pinch of salt
Olive oil

Method

1. Preheat your oven to 200°C.
2. Grease a large baking pan.
3. Remove the stems and use a spoon to gently scrape off the gills (hair) from the mushrooms.
4. Rub salt all over, including the inside.
5. Fry the garlic in olive oil for about 2 minutes.
6. Put mushrooms in the dish, upside down, and brush all over with the fried garlic.
7. Flip the mushrooms over and sprinkle some salt inside. Then fill them up with tomatoes, basil, and mozzarella pearls or grated mozzarella.
8. Sprinkle dried herbs and bake in the oven for about 10 minutes or until the mushrooms are cooked
9. Drain off any excess water
10. Enjoy!

Tips

You can use other types of mushrooms, but portobello are the steaks of the mushroom kingdom.

Any cheese of your choice is fine.

CREAM OF MUSHROOM SOUP

Ingredients

400 g canned mushroom
1/4 cup chopped onion
3 garlic cloves, chopped
2 tbsp butter
1 tbsp vegetable oil
1 cup beef broth
1 cup whipping cream
1 tbsp flour
Salt and pepper to taste

Method

1. Heat oil and butter in a saucepan and sauté garlic and onion for a minute.
2. Add mushrooms, salt, and white pepper.
3. Sauté for 2 minutes and add flour, stirring continuously.
4. Add beef broth and whipping cream while stirring continuously. Cook for another 5–7 minutes. You can add some water if you find the soup too thick.

PUMPKIN OMELETTE

Ingredients

2 tbsp olive oil
3 eggs
1/3 cup grated mozzarella cheese
1/4 cup chopped onion
1/4 cup chopped green pepper
1/4 cup sliced leeks
1/2 cup pumpkin puree
1/2 tsp oregano
1/2 tsp all-purpose seasoning
Salt to taste

Filling

1 tbsp olive oil
1 tomato, diced
1/4 cup chopped onion
1/4 cup sliced leeks
1/4 cup chopped green pepper
Salt to taste

Method

1. Heat oil in a saucepan and sauté onion, green pepper, tomato, and leeks for about 5 minutes. Add salt to taste and set aside.
2. In a medium bowl, place eggs, cheese, onion, green pepper, leeks, pumpkin puree, oregano, all-purpose seasoning, and salt to taste. Beat everything up until well blended.
3. Heat two tablespoons of oil in a large frying pan and pour egg mixture. Cook for approximately 2 minutes and flip egg over for the other side to cook.
4. Transfer omelette to a plate and sandwich with tomato filling.

OMELETTE AND CHEESE

Ingredients

4 eggs
1/3 cup grated mozzarella cheese
1/2 cup canned mushrooms, sliced
1/4 cup chopped onion
1/4 cup chopped leeks
1/2 tsp oregano
1/4 cup chopped green pepper
Salt to taste
Pepper to taste

Method

1. In a medium bowl, beat the eggs, then add cheese, mushrooms, onion, leeks, oregano, green pepper, salt, and pepper to taste. Beat everything up until well blended. Heat two tablespoons of oil in a large frying pan and pour the egg mixture. Cook for over 2 minutes and flip egg over for the other side to cook.
2. Transfer omelette to a plate and serve.

MOI MOI

Ingredients

Some ngongo leaves to tie
2 cups black-eyed beans
4 hard boiled eggs
2 uncooked eggs
2 cups water
2 red habanero peppers
1 red bell pepper
2 onions

5 spring onions
5 cloves of garlic
1 cup crayfish
1 tsp ground white pepper
¾ cup vegetable oil
1/2 kg fish, fried and deboned
Salt

Method

1. Soak beans for about 10 minutes and peel by rubbing them between your palms to take away the skin. Wash skin off by pouring plenty of water. This will enable the skin to float away and separate from the beans.
2. Blend beans with onion, garlic, red chili pepper, and red bell pepper. Pour mixture into a bowl.
3. Add salt, crayfish, white pepper, and vegetable oil and mix thoroughly. Beat two eggs and add to the mixture.
4. Cut stems from leaves and put in a pot to prevent moi moi from burning. Wash leaves thoroughly.
5. Shape leaf into a cone and pour in ¾ cup of the beans mixture. Add one-fourth of the hard-boiled egg and two small pieces of fried fish. Wrap the cone and place carefully in the pot.
6. After wrapping up all the mixture, pour two cups of boiling water into the pot and set pot on high heat. Keep topping up the water every 15 minutes and cook for over an hour.

KOKI BEANS

Ingredients

2 cups black-eyed beans, soaked, peeled, and blended
2 cups largely sliced cocoyam leaves
Pepper
2 cups water
1/2 cup palm oil
Salt to taste

Method

1. Put blended black-eyed beans in a mortar and cream for over 15–20 minutes.
2. Add salt and pepper.
3. Heat two cups of water in a saucepan, add palm oil and bring to a boil.
4. Pour water-and-oil mixture into the mortar a little at a time, while creaming the blended beans.
5. Pour it on a leaf, wrap it up and tie.
6. Line the bottom of your pot with extra leaves to prevent koki from burning up.
7. Put the tied koki bundles in a pot and put some water in the pot. Cook over high heat for about 1 1/2 hours, adding water from time to time into the pot.
8. Untie Koki and serve hot.

AKARA BEANS (BEAN CAKES)

Ingredients

2 cups black-eyed beans, soaked, peeled, and blended
1 large onion, chopped
4 cloves garlic, chopped
1/2 cup sliced green onion
Salt and pepper to taste
Vegetable oil to fry

Method

1. Mix blended beans, onion, garlic, green onion, salt, and pepper together in a medium sized bowl.
2. Pour about a litre of vegetable oil into a heavy saucepan and place on medium heat.
3. When the oil gets hot, use a spoon and drop bean mixture into the pot. Fry until golden brown, flipping it over from time to time.

PUMPKIN LEAVES

Ingredients

1 large bunch of pumpkin leaves
4 tomatoes, diced
1 onion, chopped
1 pepper, ground
1/4 cup crayfish, pounded
1/2 cup vegetable oil
Salt

Method

1. Remove all the strings from both the stems and the leaves. Rinse leaves thoroughly to remove all sand.
2. Cut stem and leaves into small pieces and boil for approximately 5 minutes. Drain and squeeze out all the water.
3. Heat oil in a saucepan and add onion and tomatoes. Stir until the tomato is cooked.
4. Add vegetable, pepper, and crayfish and mix thoroughly. Cook for a further 5–7 minutes.
5. For a slight variation, add cooked shrimps and calamari.

CABBAGE AND MUSHROOM STIR-FRY

Ingredients

1 small cabbage, cut crosswise or shredded
1 medium carrot, julienned (thin strips)
1 medium onion, chopped
1 tomato, chopped (optional)
250 g mushrooms, sliced
1 leek, sliced
2 tbsp low-sodium oyster/soy sauce
3 cloves of crushed garlic
3 tbsp vegetable oil

Method

1. Preheat a wok or skillet.
2. Pour in the oil then add the onion, garlic, and leek. Stir continuously for 2 minutes
3. Add the tomato and stir further for 3 minutes (you can skip this stage if tomato is not used).
4. Add the mushrooms and continue to stir for a further 3 minutes.
5. Finally, add the cabbage and carrots, followed by the oyster/soy sauce.
6. Mix properly until cabbage is tender and crisp.
7. Serve with a side selected from the book

CHICKEN GIZZARD KEBABS

Ingredients

500 g chicken gizzards
1 tsp white pepper
2 tsp mixed herbs and spices, blended together (basil, parsley, celery, ginger, garlic, and onions; save an extra teaspoon for brushing)
1/2 tsp paprika

1 medium seasoning cube, crushed
1 tbsp mustard (mild)
2 tbls vegetable oil
A pinch of salt
1 small onion, finely chopped
1 large onion, diced largely

Method

1. If using wooden skewers, soak them in water for at least 30 minutes. This should prevent the skewers from burning during the grilling process.
2. Clean and season the gizzards to your taste with all of the above ingredients, except the vegetable oil, the largely diced onions, and the extra teaspoon of mixed herbs and spices (for brushing).
3. Bring to a boil over low heat and allow to cook in its own juice until tender. You do not need to put any water in the pot, but ensure that the heat is medium/low to avoid burning. Stir the gizzards occasionally.
4. Once cooked, drain any water and allow to cool down.
5. Thread on a skewer, alternating between the gizzard and the largely diced onion.
6. Add the vegetable oil and a pinch of salt to the extra mixed herbs and brush on the kebabs.
7. Brush grill grates with oil, then place skewers on grill /oven/BBQ until both sides are brown.
8. Preferably served hot.

CHICKEN GIZZARD STIR-FRY

Ingredients

500 g cooked gizzards
Bell peppers (assorted colours), sliced in strips
1 onion, largely diced
1 medium tomato, chopped
50 g bean sprouts
1 tbsp low-sodium oyster sauce
1/2 tsp white pepper
freshly ground mixed herbs
Salt to taste
Vegetable oil

Method

1. Heat the oil in a pan and add the tomato. Allow to cook for a few minutes, then add the freshly ground mixed herbs and oyster sauce.
2. Next add the gizzard and continue to stir. If it looks too dry, you may add a drop of water, but not too much (about 10–15 ml).
3. Add the onion, bell peppers, and lastly, the bean sprouts. Stir continuously until veggies are cooked but crunchy.
4. Taste and add salt if necessary.

CRISPY CHICKEN IN ALMOND FLOUR (FRY OR BAKE)

Ingredients

400 g chicken thighs, bone off or on
1–2 beaten egg(s)
2 cloves garlic
1/2 tsp paprika
1/2 tsp ground basil
1/4 ground ginger

100 g almond flour (ground almond)
1/2 tsp white pepper
2 tbsp mustard (mild)
1 seasoning cube
A pinch of salt

Method

1. Skin the chicken thighs and cut into halves.
2. Place the chicken into a large bowl, season with the above ingredients (except the almond flour). Let it marinate for a couple of hours or overnight.
3. Dip the chicken into the beaten eggs and then cover generously with almond flour.
4. Deep-fry or bake until golden brown.

Tips

Almond flour is made from ground almond. You can make your own almond flour at home by putting small pieces of almond or flaked almonds in a food processor and pulsing them until they look like fine sand.

For another variation, you can coat the chicken with breadcrumbs instead of almond flour. I would recommend panko breadcrumbs as it gives an attractive look and is very crispy.

This chicken can be prepared in advance and frozen. Cook from frozen, but pay attention to the heat, especially if frying. It should be medium heat so it can cook through.

This is best eaten hot and served with salad or any side of your choice.

FISH KEBABS

Ingredients

500 g skinless, boneless fish, sliced into big chunks
1 seasoning cube, crushed
1 tsp white pepper
1/2 tsp paprika
1 tsp lemon juice

3 cloves of garlic, crushed
Salt to taste
1 onion, largely diced
1 red pepper, largely diced (you may use any colour)
10 ml vegetable oil (for brushing)

Method

1. Soak the wooden skewers in water for at least one hour to prevent them from burning on the barbeque/grill.
2. Preheat grill (electric/oven/charcoal).
3. Mix all the ingredients in a large bowl, except the fish, pepper, vegetable oil, and onion
4. Place the fish into a large bowl and pour three-fourths of the marinade over the fish.
5. Leave to marinate for at least one hour.
6. Add the vegetable oil to the remaining marinade (this is for brushing the fish).
7. Thread the fish, onion, and red pepper on the skewers and brush with the marinade.
8. Cook on your preferred grill for 8–10 minutes, turning regularly until thoroughly cooked.
9. Serve with your preferred side.

STUFFED PEPPERS

Ingredients

3 large bell peppers
200 g cooked mincemeat (follow the
steps in the cookbook on how to cook
your mincemeat)
1/2 cup chopped tomato

1 cup cauliflower rice
Grated cheese
1 tbsp vegetable oil
Salt to taste
Mixed herbs

Method

1. Pre heat your oven to 190 degrees
2. Wash and dry your peppers.
3. Cut the top off and remove the seeds.
4. Pour the vegetable oil into a large skillet and sauté the cauliflower rice for about 5 minutes, stirring from time to time.
5. Put your cooked mincemeat in a pot, then add your chopped tomatoes, cauliflower rice, mixed herbs, and salt to taste. Mix well.
6. Carefully stuff in the peppers and top with cheese.
7. Place on a greased baking dish.
8. Cover with foil and bake for about 20 minutes or until peppers are tender and cheese is melted.
9. Enjoy!

OVEN-ROASTED SPARE RIBS

Ingredients

1 kg spare ribs, cut into small pieces
1/2 tsp paprika
1/2 tsp white pepper
1 tbsp mustard (choose a mild one)
1 tbsp freshly ground mixed herbs/vegetable (basil, parsley, leeks, ginger, garlic, onion, and celery)
1 medium seasoning cube, crushed
A pinch of salt

Method

1. Put the ribs into a large bowl and add all the ingredients.
2. Mix well and allow to marinate for a couple of hours or overnight.
3. Put in an oven dish, cover with foil and place in a preheated oven (250°C) for 45 minutes.
4. Remove foil and carefully drain any excess water.
5. Return to oven until the ribs are golden brown.
6. Enjoy!

OVEN-ROASTED VEGETABLES

Ingredients (Choose Your Favourite Veggies)

1 courgette/zucchini, sliced into rings
Mixed bells peppers, largely diced
1 medium onion, largely diced
2 tbls lemon juice
2 cloves of garlic, crushed
1 medium aubergine, diced up
1 large carrot, sliced into rings

200 g mushroom
Plum/cherry tomatoes
3 tbsp olive/vegetable oil
1 tsp white pepper
Mixed dried herbs
1/2 tsp salt

Method

1. If using wooden skewers, allow to soak in water for at least 30 minutes. This prevents them from burning.
2. In a bowl, make a dressing by squeezing out the lemon juice and adding oil, crushed garlic, salt, white pepper, and mixed dried herbs. Mix well.
3. Put all the vegetables in a large bowl and pour the dressing over. Mix well and let it marinate for 30 minutes.
4. Spread the veggies on a baking sheet or roasting tin and roast until tender.

PAN-GRILLED STEAK

Ingredients

1 kg steak pieces, thinly sliced (about 8 cuts)
1 medium seasoning cube, crushed
1 tbsp freshly ground mixed herbs/vegetable (ginger, garlic, basil, parsley, celery, and onion), blended together
1 tsp black pepper
A pinch of salt
Vegetable/olive oil (you only need 2 tsp per 4 pieces)

Method

1. Put the steak pieces into a large bowl and add all the ingredients.
2. Mix well and allow to marinate for a couple of hours.
3. Heat up your skillet and add about two teaspoons of oil.
4. Put in the steak pieces and allow to cook for about 2–3 minutes on each side.
5. Garnish with mixed veggies and serve.

POULET D.G. (NO PLANTAINS)

Ingredients

1 large chicken
2 large carrots, diced
300 g green beans, cut into medium pieces and parboiled
1 large onion, chopped
2 large tomatoes, chopped
Assorted bell peppers, cut into strips

3 tbsp mixed herbs, blended together (basil, parsley, ginger, garlic, celery, and spring onions)
1 tsp white pepper
1 tsp paprika
2 medium seasoning cubes, crushed
vegetable oil
Salt to taste

Method

1. Clean and cut the chicken into small pieces.
2. Use 3/4 of the spices to season the chicken.
3. Cook the chicken until tender.
4. Put the vegetable oil into a large pot and add the chopped onions.
5. Stir continuously for about 2 minutes, then add the tomatoes and let it cook further for 4 minutes.
6. Add the parboiled green beans, followed by the carrots and the bell peppers.
7. Add the leftover spices and salt and continue to stir.
8. Add the chicken into the mixed veggies and let it simmer for a few minutes.
9. Mix well and taste, then add salt/seasoning cube if necessary.
10. Preferably served hot.

VEGETABLE KEBABS

Ingredients

1 courgette/zuchinni
Mixed bells peppers, largely diced
1 medium onion, largely diced
2 tbls lemon juice
2 cloves of garlic, crushed
1 medium aubergine
1 large carrot, sliced into rings
200 g mushrooms
Plum/cherry tomatoes
3 tbsp olive/vegetable oil
1 tsp white pepper
Mixed dried herbs
1/2 tsp salt

Method
1. If using wooden skewers, soak them in water for 30 minutes before use.
2. In a bowl, make a dressing by squeezing out the lemon juice and then adding oil, crushed garlic, salt, white pepper, and mixed dried herbs. Mix well.
3. Put all the vegetables into a large bowl, and pour the dressing over them. Mix well and let it marinate for 30 minutes.
4. Thread the veggies on the skewers and grill/roast until cooked.

Sides

SAUTÉED GREEN BEANS

Ingredients

400 g green beans, topped, tailed, and halved
2 cups beef stock
1 cup finely chopped parsley
1 onion, chopped
3 cloves garlic, chopped
1/2 tsp white pepper
Salt to taste
30 g butter

Method

1. Cook the green beans in a large pan of boiling stock until just tender, then drain.
2. Melt butter in a wok and add onion and garlic.
3. Just before they turn brown, plunge the beans and toss thoroughly. Add salt, white pepper, and parsley and stir-fry for 2 minutes.

SAUTÉED CARROTS

Ingredients

400 g carrots, cut into thin strips
1 cup beef or chicken stock
1 cup finely chopped parsley
1 onion, chopped
3 cloves garlic, chopped
1/2 tsp white pepper
Salt to taste
30 g butter

Method

1. Cook carrots in a pan of boiling stock for a few minutes (about 3–4 minutes) and then drain.
2. Melt butter in a wok and add onion and garlic. Allow to fry for 2 minutes.
3. Add carrots, white pepper, salt, and parsley. Stir-fry for 2 minutes.

SAUTÉED MUSHROOMS

Ingredients

1 can mushrooms (400 g)
2 cloves of garlic, crushed
1/3 cup finely chopped parsley
1 small onion, chopped
1/2 tsp black pepper
1 tbsp butter

Method

1. Melt butter in a wok and add onion and garlic. Stir continuously for a minute.
2. Add mushrooms, black pepper, salt, and parsley. Stir-fry for 2–3 minutes.

CARROT AND GREEN BEANS STIR-FRY

Ingredients

200 g green beans, cut into small pieces
200 g carrots, cut into small cubes
2 cups beef stock (homemade)
1 large onion, thinly sliced
3 cloves of garlic, crushed
1 tsp white pepper
1/2 cup sliced parsley
Salt to taste
2 tbsp vegetable oil

Method

1. Boil green beans in beef stock and salt until cooked (don't overcook), then drain.
2. Use the same stock to boil carrots for a few minutes (about 3–5 minutes). Drain again.
3. Heat up oil in a wok and fry onion and garlic for a minute. Just before they get brown, add cooked green beans and carrots, white pepper, and parsley. Toss for 2 minutes and serve.

CABBAGE FUFU (SWALLOW)

Ingredients

500g cabbage
Water
1tsp psyllium husk (high fibre)

Method

1. Chop up the cabbage into pieces and bring to a boil.
2. Allow to boil for approximately 10–15 minutes or until soft and tender.
3. Drain the water and puree the cabbage using a food processor/hand blender/potato masher.
4. Add the psyllium husk on to the pureed cabbage and transfer back to the cooker.
5. Stir continuously on low/medium heat for about 3 minutes until texture becomes slightly elastic.
6. Serve with your preferred soup or vegetable or wrap up to store.

Tips

You can make fufu with most vegetables using this method.

Examples include courgette/zucchini, aubergine, carrots, and spinach.

CAULIFLOWER FUFU (SWALLOW)

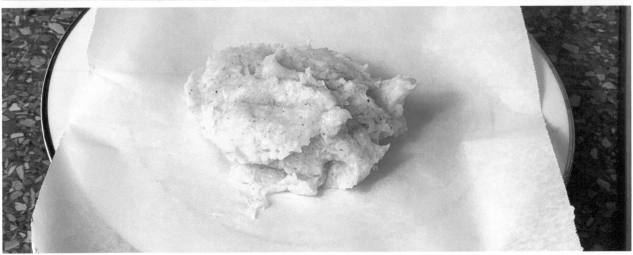

Ingredients

500g cauliflower
Water for cooking the cauliflower
1 tsp psyllium husk (high fibre)

Method

1. Cut the cauliflower head into florets and put in a pot.
2. Add enough water to cover the florets, bring to a boil and cook until cauliflower is soft.
3. Drain the water carefully and allow to cool down.
4. Put in a food processor and pulse to a pureed form or use a potato masher/hand mixer and mash till soft and smooth. This can be done in the pot which was used to cook the cauliflower.
5. Stand the pot on the burner, add the psyllium husk, and stir continuously on low heat for about 3 minutes. The texture should be a bit elastic and ready to serve or wrap up.
6. Serve with spinach/okra/eru/ or vegetable of your choice

MIXED PEPPER STIR-FRY

Ingredients

3 large bell peppers (assorted colours), cut into strips
1 medium onion
1 clove of garlic
1 tbsp low sodium soy sauce or oyster sauce (optional)
Pinch of salt
1 tbsp oil

Method

1. Heat the oil in a large frying pan or wok.
2. Put in the onion and garlic and stir continuously for a minute. Enjoy the aroma.
3. Add the mixed bell peppers, followed by your preferred sauce or salt and stir until well blended and the vegetables are tender and crisp.
4. Serve with a side of your choice.

PUMPKIN FRIES

Ingredients

Pumpkin
Salt
Vegetable oil

Method

1. Peel pumpkin and cut into little french fry shapes. Season with salt and deep-fry in a pot until they turn brown.

Snacks

CRISPY BUTTERFLY PRAWNS

Ingredients

500 g raw tiger prawns, head off, shelled, and deveined
2 beaten eggs
2 cups breadcrumbs
1/2 tsp ground white pepper
1/2 tsp garlic powder or 2 cloves of crushed garlic

Salt to taste
1/2 tsp paprika (optional)
1/2 crushed seasoning cube (optional)
2 tbsp fish sauce (optional)
Oil for deep-frying

Method

1. Put the prawns in a bowl and season with all the ingredients.
2. Dip into beaten eggs.
3. Then coat well with the breadcrumbs.
4. Deep-fry in heated oil, turning from time to time, until golden brown (about 3–5 minutes).
5. Serve hot with sweet chilli sauce or preferred dip.

Tip

If you love prawns, you will find this irresistible. This is best served hot as a starter or as part of a main meal.

(Devein prawns by removing the black line on the back, then cut prawns almost to the end, and flatten to get a butterfly shape. When peeling the shell, you can leave the tail on.)

MEATBALLS

Ingredients

500 g mincemeat (beef and pork)
1/2 tsp white pepper
1 medium onion, thinly sliced
2 cloves of garlic
4 basil leaves, ground

1/4 tsp ground ginger (preferably fresh, but powder will do)
Spring onions and/or leeks, thinly sliced
1 seasoning cube
Salt to taste
1 beaten egg

Method

1. Put the mincemeat in a bowl, add the seasoning cube and salt, and mix well.
2. Add the rest of the ingredients and mix them up well.
3. Form into balls.
4. For *steaming*, put a bit of boiled water in a pan (it has to be really shallow), then drop in the meatballs and cook for about 10 minutes, stirring from time to time.
5. For *frying*, deep-fry or shallow-fry in hot vegetable oil until golden brown.
6. For *baking*, put meatballs on a baking tray and pop in a preheated oven. Bake until golden brown.
7. Serve with some salad.

Tip

I tend to mix beef and pork fifty-fifty. You can use any kind of meat.

Use this recipe for burgers too.

SCOTCH EGGS

Ingredients

500 g sausage meat
4 hard-boiled eggs, peeled
1 beaten egg
Golden Breadcrumbs

Vegetable oil for frying
1/2 tsp ground white pepper (optional)
A pinch of salt (optional)

Method:

1. Mix up the sausage meat.
2. Add the white pepper and salt and mix well.
3. Sausage meat comes already seasoned, however, I like to enhance its taste and flavour.
4. Take a portion of the sausage meat slightly larger than the egg and spread around the egg to cover thoroughly. If the meat is too sticky, wet your hands lightly.
5. Dip the egg which has been covered in meat into the beaten egg.
6. Then roll to cover with breadcrumbs.
7. Fry in medium/hot oil until golden brown, turning from time to time.

Tip

You can also use mincemeat. Just ensure that it is finely minced and seasoned to taste. (Ginger, garlic, basil, white pepper salt, and seasoning cube are a few ingredients you may want to use.)

Then follow the steps above.

CLOUD BREAD/FLOURLESS BREAD

Cloud bread is an amazing substitute for regular bread if you are on a low-carb lifestyle. It is low in carbs and fats. It can be made plain, or you can add some seasoning, like herbs, garlic, and seeds.

Ingredients

3 large eggs, separated
1/2 tsp cream of tartar (optional)
60 g cream cheese

Pinch of salt
1/2 tsp garlic powder (optional)
1 tsp mixed herbs (optional)

Method

1. Preheat your oven to 150°C.
2. Line your baking sheets with either parchment, greaseproof, or baking paper.
3. Separate the whites from the yolks. Add the cream of tartar to the whites and beat on high until the froth turns into firm meringue peaks.
4. Place the cream cheese in a bowl and beat on medium to soften, then add the yolks and beat until the mixture is completely smooth (at this stage, you can add the garlic powder and herbs).
5. Fold in the firm meringue into the yolk mixture very gently. This process is very delicate. Be gentle in order not to deflate the meringue. Try to maintain the firm and foamy texture of the mixture.

6. Scoop out even portions of the foam on to the lined baking sheets approximately 3/4 inch high. Leave spaces around each one.
7. Bake for about 10–15 minutes until the bread is firm, golden brown, and should not wiggle when shaken.
8. Remove when cold and serve with your favourite sandwich filling.

Notes

You can store your cloud bread in an airtight container or Ziploc bag for a couple of days in the fridge or weeks in the freezer.

You can also add some sugar and sweet spices to get a dessert.

DEVILED EGGS AND HAM

Ingredients

4 hard-boiled eggs
1/4 cup thinly chopped ham
1/4 cup chopped sweet pickle
2 tbsp chopped onions
1/2 tsp white pepper
2 tbsp chopped celery

2 tbs mayonnaise
1 tsp mustard (choose a mild one)
pesto sauce (optional)
A pinch of salt
Paprika for dusting

Method

1. Slice all the eggs in half, lengthwise.
2. Carefully remove the egg yolks without breaking the whites.
3. Put the egg yolks in a bowl and mash with a fork.
4. Add the remaining ingredients and mix well.
5. Stuff the mixture into the egg white or pipe in for a more elaborate look.
6. Dust with paprika before serving.

Notes

If you love hard-boiled eggs, this will be a perfect snack for you any time of the day.

Ingredients can be substituted to one's taste. Be adventurous.

COURGETTE/ZUCCHINI PANCAKES

Ingredients

2 medium courgettes
1 egg
30 g flour (approx.2 tbsp)
Diced onion
1/2 tsp white paper
2 spring onions, sliced

Crushed seasoning cube (optional)
Salt to taste
Preferred dipping to serve
15 mlg. vegetable or olive oil to wet the
fry pan

Method

1. Grate the courgette using the large side of the grater.
2. Combine all the ingredients in a bowl and mix well.
3. Heat oil in a non-stick frying pan.
4. Use a spoon and add the mixture (three to four spoonfuls at a time depending on the size of your pancakes)
5. Shallow-fry over medium heat until golden brown on each side (2–3 minutes approximately).
6. Serve preferably hot with a dipping of your choice.

Tip

For an extra kick, add some pepper or hot chilli to the mixture before frying.

BURGERS

Ingredients

500 g mincemeat
1/2 tsp white pepper
1 medium onion, thinly sliced
2 cloves of garlic
4 basil leaves, ground

1/4 tsp ground ginger (preferably fresh, but powder will do)
spring onions and/or leeks, thinly sliced
1 seasoning cube
salt to taste
1 beaten egg

Method

1. Put the mincemeat in a bowl, add the seasoning cube and salt, and mix well.
2. Add the rest of the ingredients and mix them up well.
3. Form into tennis-sized balls and flatten the top and bottom or use a burger mould as demonstrated in the picture above.
4. For *steaming*, put a bit of boiled water in a pan (it has to be shallow), then drop in the burgers and cook for about 10 minutes, turning the sides.
5. For *frying*, shallow-fry in hot vegetable oil and fry until golden brown.
6. For *baking*, put burgers on a baking tray and pop in a preheated oven. Bake until golden brown
7. Serve with some salad or any sides.

Tip

I tend to mix beef and pork fifty:fifty. You can use any kind of meat.

This can be steamed, fried, or baked.

POACHED EGGS

Ingredients

Eggs
Salt
Pepper
1 tsp olive oil

Method

1. Grease poaching cups with olive oil.
2. Crack eggs and put each into a poaching cup.
3. Place cups over the pan with water and cover pan with lid.
4. Let egg cook over medium heat for 5–10 minutes, depending on how cooked you want your egg.
5. Remove eggs from poaching cups and serve on a plate.

Desserts

Fruits are not necessary for people on a low-carb lifestyle because they are generally very high in sugar. Too much sugar in your diet will definitely prevent ketosis. The good news is that all the nutrients in fruits can be found in vegetables. Vegetables are a better option because they do not contain all the sugar found in fruits. However, if you must eat fruits, go for a handful of raspberries, blackberries or strawberries because they are low in carbs. Other alternatives include watermelon and cantaloupe melon.

AVOCADO AND KALE SMOOTHIE

Ingredients

1/2 cup Greek yogurt
1 cup kale
½ cucumber
1 cup coconut water or plain water
1 tsp chai seeds
1 tsp ginger
1/2 cup ripe avocado
1/2 lemon
Ice cubes (optional)

Method

1. Put all ingredients in a blender and blend until smooth.
2. You can add more coconut water/water to thin out the smoothie.

BERRY SMOOTHIE

Ingredients

- 1 cup Greek yogurt
- 1/2 cup coconut water/water
- 1/4 cup blueberries
- 1/4 cup raspberries
- 1 tsp chia seeds
- Ice cubes (optional)

Method

1. Put all ingredients in a blender and blend till smooth.
2. Serve immediately or refrigerate until ready to serve.

CLASSIC GREEN JUICE

Ingredients

1 cucumber
1 cup spinach
2 celery stalks
1/2 or 1 lemon

Method

1. Squeeze the lemon into the juicer whilst removing the seeds.
2. Put all ingredients in a juicer and extract the juice.
3. Serve immediately or refrigerate until it's time to serve.

Notes

This juice is suitable for home freezing.

CRÈME FRAICHE DELIGHT

Ingredients

1/2 cup crème fraiche
2 blackberries
2 raspberries
2 strawberries, sliced in half

Method

1. Spoon the crème fraiche into a dessert bowl and top with berries.
2. Serve immediately or refrigerate until you are ready to serve it.

MELON BALLS FRUIT SALAD

Ingredients (Choose Your Favourite Melons)

Watermelon
Cantaloupe melon
Santa Claus melon

Method

1. Wash and dry the melons.
2. Cut melons into two halves.
3. Use a spoon and gently remove the seeds.
4. Use a melon baller and scoop out the melons into small balls.
5. Serve and enjoy or refrigerate until you are ready to serve it.

SIMPLY WATERMELON

Ingredient

1 watermelon

Method

1. Wash and dry the watermelon.
2. Cut into half, lengthwise.
3. Then cut each half into another half.
4. You should now have 4 pieces
5. Slice each quarter into thin slices and place on a platter
6. Serve or keep in the fridge until you are ready to serve it

STRAWBERRY AND GREEK YOGURT DESSERT

Ingredients

1 cup Greek yogurt
1/4 tsp chai seeds
3 strawberries, cut in halves

Method

1. Pour the Greek yogurt in a dessert bowl.
2. Top with strawberries and chai seeds.

WHIPPED CREAM HEAVEN

Ingredients

50 ml double cream (whipped)
1/4 cup raspberries
1/4 cup blueberries
2 strawberries, halved
1 tsp organic cocoa powder (unsweetened)

Method

1. Pour the cream into a little bowl and add the cocoa powder.
2. Whip the cream to piping consistency.
3. Pipe into your dessert bowl and top with berries.

Lightning Source UK Ltd.
Milton Keynes UK
UKHW051404221119
354013UK00003B/94/P